To Pamela —

Your daughter Tanesha loves you VERY MUCH, but God loves you more!

Happy Mother's Day!

♡ Everydice ♱

Grace

9 MAY 10

Acclaim for God's Grace:

God's Grace

Psalms of Love, Laughter, Tears and Praise from Mother to Daughter

By Grace's Mommy—
Major Eurydice S. Stanley, Ph.D.

CG Christian Grace
PUBLISHING
- St. Augustine, Florida -

God's Grace:
Psalms of Love, Laughter, Tears and Praise from Mother to Daughter

Text Copyright ©2006 by Eurydice S. Stanley
Illustrations and graphics property of Christian Grace Publishing

TM & © Copyright 2006, Christian Grace Publishing

All scriptural references are from the King James Version of the Holy Bible.

Christian Grace Publishing titles may be purchased for counseling, business, promotional use or for special sales. For information, please write the address above or visit our web site at www.christiangracepublishing.com.

Christian Grace Publishing and its logo, a letter C with a heart and a letter G with a cross, are trademarks of Christian Grace Publishing.

First edition published 2006

Library of Congress Cataloging-in-Publication Data
Stanley, Eurydice
God's Grace: Psalms of Love, Laughter, Tears and Praise from Mother to Daughter
Eurydice Stanley
1. Motherhood. 2. Poetry 3. Parenting - Religious aspects-Christianity 4. Family & Relationships - Parenting 5. Family and Relationships - General 6. Religion - Inspirational 7. Religion - Spirituality

ISBN 0-9774468-0-8
13 Digit ISBN 978-09774468-0-3

Library of Congress Control Number: 2005909394

Printed in the United States of America

Christian Grace
PUBLISHING

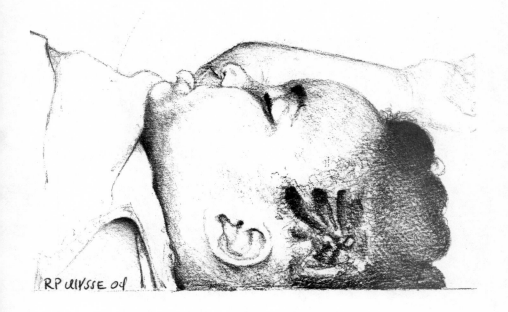

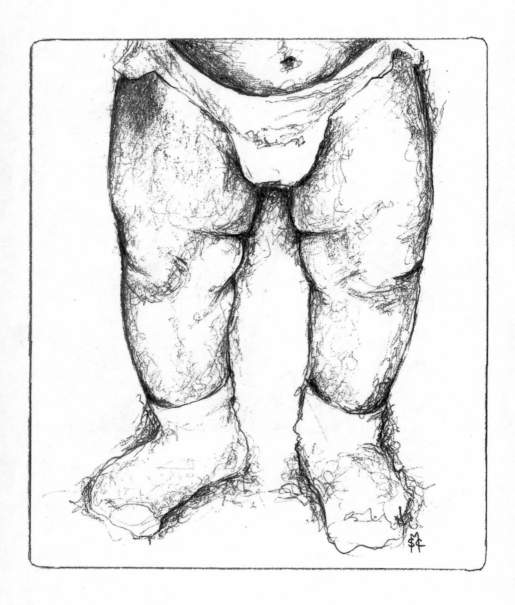

WITH SINCERE APPRECIATION…

Lord, I pray the words you entrusted me with are properly reflected on these pages…
I give this work back to you.

To the Special Women I've been blessed with in my life:

FOR GRACE, My Daughter, My Love, My God-Given Purpose for Life!

For my Mommy Priscilla, I will always be appreciative of her pride in being my Mother
and for calling me "Her First and Her Bestest"
(Although I know you said the same thing to all of us!)

For Grandma Mitchell and Grandma Rozelle…thank you for your personal sacrifices
and for providing our family with a strong example of matriarchic love and dedication.

For the many wonderful women who have taken me under their wing through the years
(there are too many to list) thank you for your love, support and example!

For Grace's loving relatives, the Mitchell, Rozelle, Luke, Greer, Stephens, Walls, Wofford,
Nettles, Barazza, Johnson, Eli, Tasby, and Edwards families.

It definitely takes a village to raise a child, and we've been blessed with people who
loved Grace sight unseen and overwhelmed us with concern since conception -
God-given Grandmas and Grandpas Joe, Lambright and Starr; Loving Aunts and
Uncles Nichols,Lamar, Watts, Threets, Collins, Eargle, and Boone.

For the girlfriends who supported me and accepted my frantic calls at all hours of the
day or night – Clarisa, Sue, Carla, Kathy, Sonya, Dina, Deidra, Enika and Adriene –
thanks for your patience and support – and for making me laugh!

For the many caring souls who reviewed this manuscript and provided great advice -
Laurie Z., Aunt Lenita, Mark, Que-Que, Pastor Arlene, Pastor Jon, Dave and Mrs. Henry.

Grace has a legion of blessed bodyguards, to include her Daddy Shon, my brothers
Que and Aaron, Uncle Mickey, new baby brother Christian and Paw-Paw Stephens.

Thanks to Father-figures who showed me unconditional love, mentorship and support
(whether they realized it or not)
Uncle Joe, Uncle Hendricks, Uncle Curtis, Doc Taylor, Uncle Jon and Daddy Starr

THERE ARE TOO MANY LOVING PEOPLE TO RECOGNIZE,
IF YOU ARE NOT LISTED ON THIS PAGE, YOU ARE IN MY HEART!
I THANK GOD FOR YOU ALL –
CONTINUED BLESSINGS!

The Spirit itself beareth
witness with our spirit,
that we are the
children of God

Romans 8:16

FEED
THE CHILDREN

**FIFTY PERCENT OF THE PROCEEDS FROM THIS BOOK
WILL BENEFIT THE FOLLOWING
FEED THE CHILDREN PROGRAMS:**

**GULFCOAST HURRICANE VICTIMS
(OPERATION KATRINA)**

ABC ABANDONED BABY CENTERS IN AFRICA

MILITARY FAMILIES

**DIRECT CONTRIBUTIONS TO FEED THE CHILDREN
CAN BE MADE BY CALLING 1.800.627.4556.**

*"...feed the flock of God which is among you, taking the oversight thereof,
not by constraint, but willingly..."*
1 Peter 5:2

Contents

Introduction	15
You Are Being Evicted!	19
Important Introductions	21
Shhh…the Baby is Sleeping	23
Nursing Blues	25
Yes, I'm a Princess	27
My Precious Jewel	29
Thank You	31
Looking Through The Eyes of a New Mommy	33
Readiness Rations	35
Well Developed	36
Crying Over Spilled Milk	37
Sweet Butterfly Kisses	39
Sleepytown	41
Everybody Loves You	43
Waddle Walk	45
Soulmates	47
Could Anything Be Better?	48
Baby Psychology	49
She's So Sweet!	51
I Pray For You	53
I'm So Proud of You	55
What A Smile!	57
Thankful	59
Lazy Afternoon	61
What Happened to This Room?	63
Precious	65
Perfection	67
Complete Comprehension	69
She Just Is…	71
Kissing the Hurt Away	72
Peace on Earth	73
Interruption	75
When I Knew You Were Mine	76
What's Next?	77
Diva	79
Yay, It's Naptime!	81
Perfect Lips	83
Manicures and Pedicures	84
Where's My Camera?	85
You're More Than Enough	87
A Christmas to Remember	89
Dance With Mommy	91

Contents (cont.)

Manna From Heaven	93
Snuggling With Mommy	94
Essence Of My Baby	95
Time To Wean The Baby	97
Captured Kisses	99
My Angel	101
Adventures in Restauranting	102
Mimic	103
Extended Family	105
New Teeth	106
Who Are Godparents?	107
Stop It!	109
Brown Sugar	111
Amazing	113
Heritage of Love	115
What Are You Doing?	116
"Gifts In My Glass"	117
You Are Perfect For Nibbling!	119
A Warning To The Babysitter	120
Big Hug!	121
I Promise	123
War May Call	125
"Ambrosia"	127
Happy Easter, Sunshine	128
Happily Snowed In	129
A Visit To The Doctor	131
My Mother's Day Gift	133
Colic Blues	135
Heartbeat	137
Happy Birthday, Sweetheart!	139
"The Oneness"	141
Baby Sandwich	143
Cry	145
The Daddy-Daughter Connection	147
Baby Fulfillment	149
You're Incredible	151
No!	152
As It Should Be	153
Daddy's Girl Mommy's Baby	155
What A Performance!	156
Where Are You Going, Busy Bee?	157
Wonderful	158

Contents (cont.)

Life Long Friends	159
Learning Through You	161
Through A Daughter's Eyes	163
Mommy's Life Force	164
Store Investigations…Stay With Mommy!	165
Every Day Is Sweeter	167
Parts Make A Great Whole!	169
Strong Sense of Ownership	170
Grace is Mommy's Baby	171
Mommy's Home	173
Daycare Drama	174
Perfect Proportions	175
Trinity of Love	177
Cooties Galore	178
Grace Is…	179
Liquefied Dinner	180
Family Fun Day	181
Accomplishment	182
Miss Independence	183
Thank You, Father	185
Your Greatness Has Been Prophesied!	187
Should Anything Ever Happen	189
For Grace	191
Epilogue	193
A Special Invitation	195
About the Author	197
About the Artists	199

Introduction

This compilation is an effort to help parents give voice to their feelings of love. Consider each poem a reflection of both a parent's love for their child and Christ's love for us. This is a labor of love, is a dismal attempt to voice my overwhelming feelings for my child. They chronicle the life of Grace, my firstborn, from pregnancy to 2 years of age. I started writing when I discovered my prenancy 6 months to the day after 9/11 - I was supposed to be at the Pentagon that day due to work but kept being delayed at my office! My husband finally consented to start trying to have a child after the trauma of that experience - little did we know how much we had been missing and how Grace would change our entire world!

There is nothing like a parent's love - definitely reinforced since Grace's birth! My love for my child strenghened my love for Father God. Pastor Jon Eargle provided the best visualization of God during a sermon...as he spoke, I could see God as my "Daddy," laughing with delight at everything I did...a proud Papa who kissed my knee when it was scraped and comforted me when I was upset. God's love and care for us does not end simply because we're out of diapers...the older we get, the more we need Him and the more He avails Himself to us! As earthly parents, we are privileged to have the example of the best parent in the world – God, who serves as both Mother and Father to our eternal inner child.

Many circumstances in my life have changed since writing this book (we've even been blessed with another child, a beautiful son named Christian who will forever remind us of the 2004 Florida Hurricane Season!), but though trials come and situations change, the love and joy of parenting remains constant. So it is for our relationship with God.

My daughter, a wonderful muse, made the writing of these poems effortless, but I continued to lose track of them since most were written on whatever was closest to me when I was "inspired"... napkins, paper bags, anything that was handy! The majority were written while I was separated from Grace due to work – the verses helped me feel close to her until I returned home. I've actually lost more poems than those represented in this collection!

The prospect of publishing for a Type A personality such as myself was paralyzing until my former Pastor, Lyle Dukes, encouraged me to release the words God had given to me. He reminded me that the words before you are not mine, rather another present to compliment God's wonderful gift, our sweet daughter.

I pray these "Psalms of Love and Grace" mirror the love you hold for your child or children, or remind you of a joy you may have lost along the way....children truly are a reflection on earth of the love God has for each one of us, His precious babies!

Enjoy and Continued Blessings!

...And He said unto me,
My grace is
sufficient for thee:
for my strength is made
perfect in weakness.
Most gladly will I rather
glory in my infirmities,
that the power of Christ
may rest upon me.

II Corinthians 12:9

For Grace and Christian...
My sweet Princess and Prince...
Mommy loves you always!

In Loving Memory of Model Mothers...

Beloved Grandma Emmazhaye P. Mitchell &
Mrs. Julie Moore, Army Wife and Mother...

Please continue to
shower love from heaven!

Lo, children are an heritage of the Lord: and the fruit of the womb is His reward.

Psalm 127:3

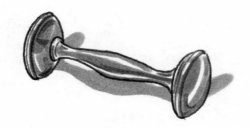

You Are Being Evicted!

Excuse me, little baby,
But your time is well past due-
I am presenting an eviction notice to you!

You've borrowed my body long enough –
You've distorted it beyond any sight ever seen...
Get out now - enough is enough
This is not a good start, child - I will soon become gruff!

Two weeks overdue
And over twenty hours of labor endured,
Clearly we know you are in charge-
Now just come out and take over the world at large!

I've begged, I've pleaded -
Come out of me!
Give Mommy some relief –
Truly, I'm not being selfish - please respond to my need!

I long to see you,
And hold you close to me,
Come on out, Sweet baby-
No more love internally!

©Eurydice Stanley

Greet one another
with a kiss of charity.
Peace be with you all
that are in Christ Jesus.
Amen.

1 Peter 5:14

Important Introductions

Our baby is coming -
    What will I say?
        When we meet on her very first birthday?

I look horrendous -
    My hair is a fright,
        And my face is flushed from screaming throughout the night!

Will she like me?
    Will she see…
        Everything she hoped for in a new Mommy?

Regardless, I'll love her-
    And I'll always strive to be,
        The very best possible Mommy!

Hello Baby!
    You're beautiful as can be!
        It's so good to see you – finally!

© Eurydice Stanley

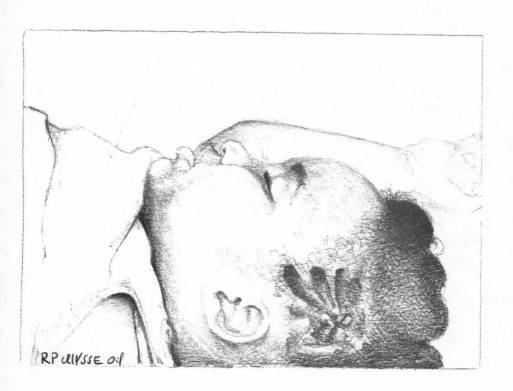

RP ulysse 09

Shhhh....the Baby is Sleeping

Shhhh...the baby is sleeping...and Mommy watches...
   Caring for her all through the night (just like the day)...
      Rocking her to sleep...
         Soothing her should she awake...
            Watching her breath dance,
                  Her chest rising and lowering in sync with the
                    angels pirouetting about her head.

I thank God as I wonder at the miracle of you, Baby...
   From your beautiful long eyelashes which kiss your cheeks,
      To the secret smile that crosses your lips from pleasant dreams.

I kiss you, smelling your lavender scented hair and skin,
   Your breath as sweet and warm as your heart.

I marvel at how perfect you are,
   From your curly hair,
      To your plump toes,
         And all the juicy, beautiful rolls in between...

Each fold providing hours of fun for Mommy, who ensures every spot
   is covered in kisses daily...

The best job in the whole wide world!

I look forward to the same gainful employment with each new sunrise,
   my Sunshine...

Until then...
   Shhh....the baby is sleeping...and Mommy watches...

© Eurydice Stanley

23

As newborn babes,
desire the sincere
milk of the Word,
that ye may
grow thereby...
1 Peter 2:2

Nursing Blues

(Dedicated to Model Milking Mommy Kathy!)

For a new Mommy,
Each drop of milk can be a battle of resistance –
Often fought against a breastpump, the bane of my existence!

How does this thing work?
I only pumped an ounce or two?
My child will starve to death, I'm sure - Nurse, what am I to do?

Hungry again little one?
You just ate an hour ago!
I don't know if I have anything left – but I'm willing to give it a go!

Ouch! Please don't bite!
Wow, what a powerful suck!
Hopefully, I'll still have skin left on my breast when you're finished
  (with any luck!)

Nurse, what do you mean that I'm engorged?
Get these rocks off my chest!
My baby can't latch on this way, and my terrified husband doesn't know
  what to do or say!

Cabbage leaves? What? How? Why?
They go where?
Whatever it takes to make this pain go away, Nurse, I don't care!

OK, OK, I'll try again –
My baby must have the best,
You'd better believe I'll do what it takes - I am up to this test!

Hmmm, this isn't so bad…look at her, she smiled!
Ahhh, the burp of satisfaction,
Mommy's first official meal for her child!

We'll make this happen, Baby, trust me, we will!
The two of us together with the Lord on our side -
The rest is downhill!   © Eurydice Stanley

But ye are a
chosen generation,
a royal priesthood,
a holy nation,
a peculiar people,
that ye should shew
for the praises of Him
who hath called you
out of darkness into
His marvelous light.

1 Peter 2:9

Yes, I'm a Princess!
(For Auntie Clarisa and Uncle Walt – True Royalty!)

Yes, I'm a Princess –
    Both my Daddy's are Kings,
        And I enjoy the favor their special status brings.

As a child of the Heavenly King
    I am heir,
        To treasures beyond imagination,
            And intrinsic riches beyond compare!

My Heavenly Father created all,
    And said I am His seed –

My earthly Daddy provides guidance and monitors my every step,
    He provides two strong arms to hold on to during my time of need.

My Mommy is a Queen -
    And prepares me to take my rightful place on the throne –

My riches are not measured by wealth,
    But by love and happiness alone!

I'm a royal heir –
    My parents come from a royal, heavenly line,
        Ensuring I'll have thousands of blessings
            from now until the end of time!

Hope this clarifies my lineage -
    And explains why I seem,
        Happy all the time,
            and filled with joy and glee!

Yes, I'm blessed by birthright and faith-
    But my blessings can be yours too!
        Confess faith in God – give Him your life -
          And you'll be royalty too!

© Eurydice Stanley

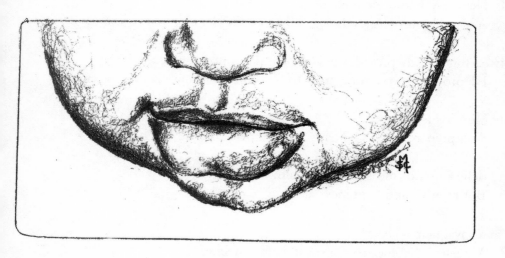

My Precious Jewel

Onyx eyes,
Ruby red lips,
Topaz skin,
Nails with opal tips…

You're a precious jewel…your treasures are yet to be discovered!

A champagne diamond unmasked,
Surviving nine months of pressure and darkness
You came out to the light shining,
Sparkling,
Incredibly captivating –
Every single facet of you.

Your Daddy and I watch in wonder,
Cherishing each brilliant sparkle
As we lovingly lift you on a pedestal of pride for display to the world…
A pedestal from which you will never come down, Sweet Princess.

Shine on,
Priceless, precious jewel –

Dazzle the world!

© Eurydice Stanley

I thank thee, O Father, Lord of heaven and earth, because thou hast hid these things from the wise and the prudent, and hast revealed them unto babes.

Matthew 11:25

Thank You

There's that secret smile,

    The special one you save for Mommy…

        Once again you reel me in…

            What a privilege to share your world!

Thank You, God, for my Special Girl!

Vanity of vanities
...all is vanity...
Ecclesiastes 1:2

Looking Through the Eyes of a New Mommy
(Dedicated to Cousin Andrea, Supermom!)

Wooden stairs, once elegant, now set off alarms,
    Looking through the eyes of a new Mommy.

Marble flooring, once opulent, no longer has charm,
    Looking through the eyes of a new Mommy.

Glamour and style used to be the theme,
    Now home safety makes me beam!
        Looking through the eyes of a new Mommy.

Hide the scissors!
    Secure the glass!
        Move away from the stove!
            Cover that plug fast!
                Baby protection and safety are key -
                Looking through the eyes of a new Mommy.

Cluttered rooms have become the norm,
    (the family room is routinely hit by a baby hurricane storm!)
        As long as the chaos is safe and germ-free, what's the harm?
        Looking through the eyes of an *exhausted* new Mommy!

© Eurydice Stanley

My God
shall supply all
your needs according to
His riches in glory
by Christ Jesus.

Philippians 4:19

Readiness Rations

Not wanting to be caught unprepared
I'd collect baby goods incessantly,
My diaper bag eventually held enough items
To meet 10 children's needs!

Slice of cheese,
Pretzels galore,
Jar of creamed peas,
I'm sure we'll need more!

Powdered formula,
Just in case,
Distilled water,
Apple-pear juice to taste.

Two sets of extra clothes-
Diapers, wipes, changing pad,
Oh my, I can't carry this heavy bag –
Little one, where is your Dad?

I didn't want to be caught unprepared, but that seems an impossible deed –
I seemed to always leave something I *thought* the baby would need…
That huge bag became nothing but cumbersome and embarrassing -
I hope, dear Father, you have forgiven my lack of faith for your provision
        and hoarding greed!

What wasted time and energy
Spent on a bag -
When the world's children have needs,
Lord willing, my child will never have.

Lord, thank you for provisions
That many children don't share,
Remind me to be ever thankful for our blessings
And to keep all the world's children in prayer!

© Eurydice Stanley

Well Developed

I've been perusing several books on "baby psychology,"

And I've determined that if love is the basis of development,

    And kisses the impetus for growth,

        And hugs the stimulus for happiness...

Then you, sweet baby, will be a happy, well-adjusted, statuesque genius!

Crying Over Spilled Milk

Whoever said "Don't cry over spilled milk" never attempted to produce
    Life sustenance for a beloved child
        in the form of body-pumped juice!
They never wailed as scab encrusted nipples were prodded,
    pumped and coaxed,
        Blistered atop breasts engorged awaiting release,
           from a baby, a cabbage leaf,
                anything that would cause the pain to cease!
Determined, I continued to breastfeed,
    Setting small goals that would gradually build…
        After one week of nursing I'd rationalize – at least she'll have the
           all-important colostrums and antibodies - next week I
           might have to yield…
OK, I'll try this for two weeks,
    Which eventually became a month, and then two,
        Soon Mommy and Baby had the hang of it
        and we knew just what to do!
Small victories were celebrated – Whoo-Hoo we pumped an ounce!
    Wasted milk by daycare or Daddy would cause Mommy to pounce!
Supplements were taken to increase milk production and flow,
    I prayed that the baby would be full after nursing
        and her rosy cheeks would glow!
Each ounce was a victory – double digits were a rave,
    But seemingly the more milk produced, the more the baby craved!
Gadgets were purchased to pump milk galore-
    I really wasn't prepared for what was in store!
I just knew that each drop of milk was not to be taken for granted,
    Because it nourished our baby and kept her strong –
        Prayers for an abundant milk flow were sent
        up to Heaven all day long!
So please don't lecture me regarding crying over milk spilt –
    I know of what I speak –
        Although I (with God's help) eventually
           achieved "Lactation Nirvana,"
                My mountain of strain reached its peak!
I'd do it all again in a heartbeat, however –
    The bond with my baby cannot be matched –
        The life sustenance proved invaluable to baby's health
        And Mommy's frantic tears dried up fast!

© Eurydice Stanley

Sweet Butterfly Kisses

Your long curved eyelashes reach the sky,

Perfect for butterfly kisses from your eye!

Since you're still young,

Mommy will ensure

That your sweet Butterfly Kisses come from her!

I say "Butterfly Kisses" and you giggle with glee,

Because you know you'll soon be tickled by Mommy!

I pull you close and whisper in your ear

"Butterfly Kisses are here!"

Flit, Flutter, Flutter -

You delightedly squeal - another kiss landed!

Yet another successful attack by Mommy,

"The Butterfly Kiss Bandit!"

© Eurydice Stanley

Come unto me,
all ye that labor
and are heavy laden,
and I will give you rest.
Take my yoke upon you,
and learn of Me,
for I am meek
and lowly in heart:
And ye shall find rest
for your souls,
for My yoke is easy
and My burden is light.

Matthew 11:28–30

Sleepytown

Off to sleep you go -

    The angels all come down,

        They will escort you **back to heaven** to visit home,

            You're no longer earth-bound!

Sleepytown, Sleepytown -

    Go on off to play!

        Time to get your rest -

            Tomorrow is **another big day!**

© Eurydice Stanley

Beloved, let us
love one another
for love is of God.

1 John 4:7

Everybody Loves You
(A song originally created for Uncle Aaron, my first baby!)

Everybody loves you,
Everybody loves you,
But not as much as I do.

I love you in the spring,
In the summertime and the fall,
I love you in the winter,
       When the little snowflakes fall! Oh!

Everybody loves you,
Everybody loves you,
But not as much as I do.

You're the sunshine of my life,
You make me happy in every way,
You've got such a lovely spirit,
That all I have to say, is -

Everybody loves you,
Everybody loves you,
But not as much as I do!

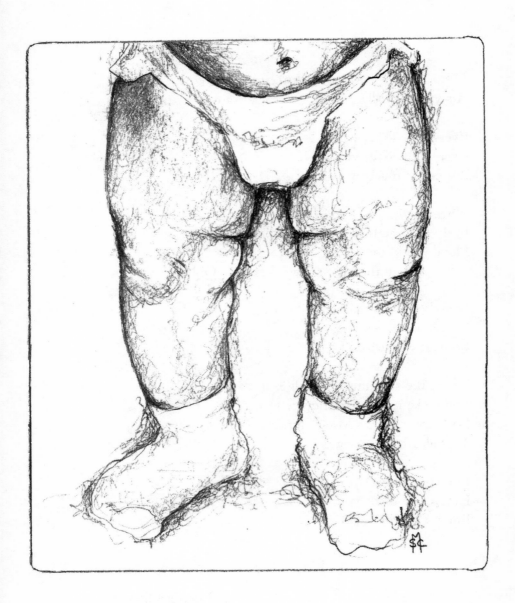

Waddle Walk

Waddle, Walk,

Waddle, Walk,

Bobble to and fro,

Pause to pick up paper -

    Then off again you go!

Waddle, Walk,

Waddle, Walk,

Now you're on your way —

Soon you will be running,

    Waddle on today!

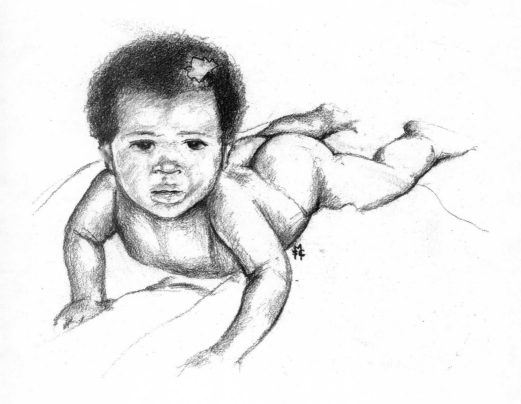

Soulmates

How could it be...

That this tiny little person could represent so much of me?

My Soulmate.

Born of my flesh and flesh of my soul-

Your indomitable spirit shines forth-

Our family is now whole.

Our Soulmate.

You've stolen our hearts and kept the key –

A reflection of your parent's love and faith, beautifully...

God's Soulmate.

You are a reflected image of our past-

A vision of hope for the future –

A beautiful, brilliant Angel who makes our hearts soar!

Who could've known what God had in store?

Soulmates-

Thank you Lord, forevermore!

© Eurydice Stanley

Could Anything Be Better?

Could anything be better than being this child's Mother?

Could anything be better than seeing her wait for me by the door
    when I come home?

Could anything be better than having her reach for me to pick her up?

Could anything be better than a sweet, close hug as the baby
    pats my back?

Could anything be better than a sweet kiss of pure love?

Could anything be better than hearing MaMa and DaDa all day long?

Could anything be better than hearing my baby
    laugh and giggle with glee?

Could anything be better than a special smile just for Mommy?

Could anything be better than special "quiet" time-
    just the baby and me?

Could anything be better than watching a new tooth make its way out?

Could anything be better than hearing a new word?

Could anything be better than discovering a new skill?

Could anything be better than changing a diaper,
    knowing everything is working inside baby?

Could anything be better than our "Girls Day Out,"
    special bonding time together?

Could anything be better than squeals of delight?

Could anything be better than spontaneous dancing to "muzak"
    in store aisles?

Could anything be better than prancing proudly in a new outfit,
    like the Princess that you are?

    ...On second, thought, no...not ever...nothing could be better!

© Eurydice Stanley

Baby Psychology

If it's closed, I'll open it!

If it's sealed, I'll break in!

If it's within reach, I'll take it!

Everything is mine –

Don't you know who always wins?

If I see it, I want it,

If you say no, I want it more!

I really don't know how to write yet, but I'll try…

On the wall, the carpet, your important papers, even the sky!

If you want me to eat it, I won't,

If you *don't* want me to eat it, I will…

Who said being a Mommy would be easy?

Every exciting, unpredictable baby step is uphill!

© Eurydice Stanley

*How sweet are
your words
to my taste,
Sweeter than honey
to my mouth!*
Psalm 119:103

She's So Sweet

She's So Sweet —

But she's sweetest when I hold her close as she sleepily alternates
between nursing, caressing my breast and sleeping…

She's So Sweet —

But she's sweetest as she chases after Daddy, her best friend, confidant,
protector and love of her life.

She's So Sweet —

But she's sweetest when I catch her staring at me, as she turns her head
to the side as if to say "I *see* you, Mommy", or, if I've done something
off the wall, her look says "It's OK, that's just my Mommy!"

She's So Sweet —

But she's sweetest when we're getting dressed for church and she sits
there amazingly beautiful in a new outfit that will never be worn again
because next week there's another new outfit she'll look fabulous in…

She's So Sweet —

But she's sweetest when she provides "Sugar on Request", the sweetest
kisses ever imagined!

She's So Sweet —

But she's sweetest as a busy bee, discovering one treasure after the next
throughout the house to share (*or not!*) with Mommy and Daddy…

She's So Sweet —

But she's sweetest when she is what she'll always be —
My Baby, My Sweetheart, forever a part of me!

© Eurydice Stanley

The effectual fervent prayer of a righteous man availeth much.

James 5:16

I Pray For You
(For Pastor and Sister Riley)

I pray for you...
      That you'll know the Lord as your Father and Friend,
           For He will *always* be with you, even until the end.

I pray for you...
      That you'll ask daily for God's guidance and light,
           Constantly asking Him to show you what is right.

I pray for you...
      That your path will always be clear, if not straight,
           Leading you to the Heavenly gates.

I pray for you...
      That your going will be consistent, if not easy,
           And your rewards will be great, if few.

I pray for you...
      That your inner strength and fortitude will remain,
           although challenges come your way.

I pray for you...
      That you'll always know love
           And be able to discern,
                 The intentions of others
                     For whom your heart yearns.

I pray for you...
      That you'll use money wisely
           Not as a crutch,
                 To replace unfulfilled needs
                     that really don't matter much.

I pray for you...
           Everyday...

© Eurydice Stanley

Words of the wise,
spoken quietly,
should be heard
rather than the shout
of a ruler of fools.

Ecclesiastes 9:17

I'm So Proud Of You

(Inspired by GrandDaddy Starr)

When you look back on your life, my child -
Never regret what you could've been done,
Be grateful for what you did, my Sweet!
As a life filled with doubt can never be complete.

Remember life's simple pleasures,
Innocent from within.
Express and seek true love -
That's where true fulfillment begins.

You are a precious, perfect flower that blossoms everyday!
My charge from God is to nurture you and shower you with love;
  I am to ensure your proper growth,
    and teach you right from wrong,
      I'm tasked to lead you properly
        To ensure that you grow strong.

My prayer is that you'll be discerning, respectful and dignified with
  personal pride so no one will lead you astray -
    That you'll keep your eyes on the Lord,
      And let Him lead the way.

Baby, maintain your vision and your goals -
    Do not be deterred,
        Realize life will throw you many a curve.

Stand your ground, Honey,
    Say to any mountain of conflict "Be Thou Removed"
      And if not -
        Go over, under, around or through!

I'm so proud of you, Dear, and always will be -
    Remember I loved you then,
      I love you now,
        I'll always give thanks to God for you,
          Unconditionally, no matter what you do!
            © Eurydice Stanley

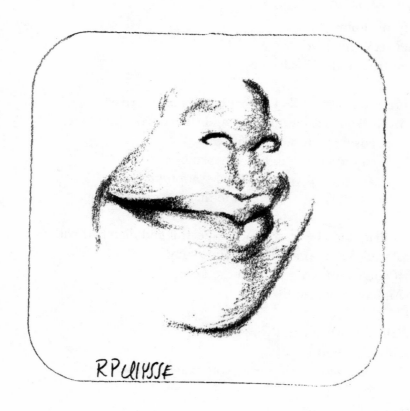

RPUlysse

What a Smile!

Hidden treasures lie behind

The light within your eyes

What a smile!

You look at me as if to say

You know me in every way,

What a smile!

You make grey skies blue

With your love forever true,

I could never do without you

And that big, beautiful smile!

© Eurydice Stanley

Enter into His gates
with thanksgiving,
And into His courts
with praise.
Be thankful to Him
and bless His name.
For the Lord is good;
His mercy is everlasting,
And His truth endureth
to all generations.
Psalm 100:4-5

Thankful

Cheek on my chest,
You nuzzle my breast,
It's time for a midnight snack.

You pause for a smile,
And babble awhile,
Face aglow by the firelight.

Oh what joy you bring,
My heart sings,
Each time I look at your sweet face.

Soon you nod off to sleep,
Leaving me to cry silently,
Thank you, Father God, for this wonderful Blessing!

© Eurydice Stanley

*This is the day that
the Lord has made.
Let us rejoice
and be glad in it.*

Psalm 118:24

Lazy Afternoon

I chew on your neck,
    You giggle and push me away,
        Then you lean your head back,
            Inviting more as if to say,
                "Mommy, come play!"

So I take the bait,
    And nibble again,
        You giggle and laugh –
            May this afternoon of fun never end!

© Eurydice Stanley

He maketh
the barren women
to keep house,
and to be a joyful
mother of children.
Praise ye the Lord.
Psalm 112:9

What Happened to This Room?

How did these toys seemingly jump out?

     And the furniture become toppled all about?

How were these clothes strewn across the floor -

     Paper and junk from door to door?

Oh My!

You have a special skill, little girl…

     You can demolish a room in two seconds flat,

          But then you smile and stare innocently for awhile –

     Who could be upset with that?

© Eurydice Stanley

Finally, brethren,
whatsoever
things are true,
whatsoever
things are just,
whatsoever
things are pure,
whatsoever
things are lovely,
whatsoever things are
of good report;
if there be any virtue,
and if there be any praise,
think on these things.

Philippians 4:8

Precious

You're so precious -

    A special gift,

        A treasure,

            Sweeter than sweet,

                More than love,

                    Greater than anything this world has to offer -

                Our life,

                Our joy,

                Precious.

© Eurydice Stanley

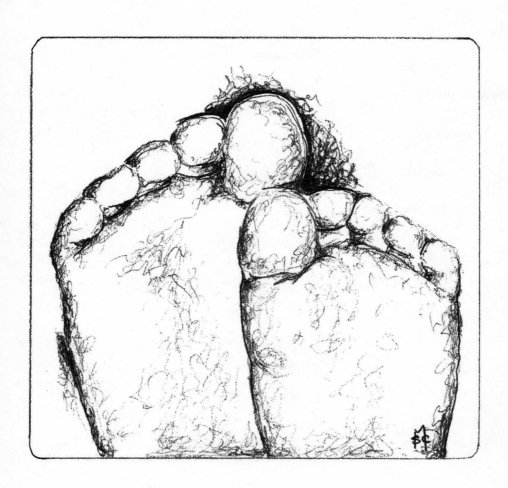

Perfection

Tiny feet,

Tiny toes,

And a perfect button nose.

Smiles that brighten up my day,

I'm so glad you came our way!

Perfection, pure and simple!

© Eurydice Stanley

Children, obey your parents in all things; for this is well pleasing unto the Lord.

Colossians 3:20

Complete Comprehension

You look at me intently,

Hanging on every word,

Nothing I say is beyond your comprehension or attention

Unless I say...

No!

Stop!

Don't!

Put that Down!

Then a fog covers your eyes and you suddenly don't understand,

Busily trying to complete my deterring command!

Sweetie, you can't fool Mommy...

I know you understand!

© Eurydice Stanley

...and a little child shall lead them.
Isaiah 11:6

She Just Is...

(For Uncle Curt and Auntie Willie Mae - Mommy knows she gets it honest!)

She's not spoiled-
She's well-loved,
What else should one expect?

She's not hard-headed-
She's determined,
She'll complete any self-directed task.

She's not unfriendly-
She's reserved,
She'll love you when her test is passed.

She's not self-absorbed-
She's driven,
She'll get to desired destinations fast.

She's not aggressive,
She's assertive,
She knows what she wants!

She's not petite,
She's a strong Amazon,
Yet her strength she never flaunts.

She's not a follower,
She's a leader,
Others are drawn to her inner light.

She's not a fighter,
She's protective,
She'll shield loved ones with all her might.

She's not stubborn-
She's strong-willed,
She'll always stand her ground...

She's simply my Princess,
She's Perfection...
She's the Best All-Around!

© Eurydice Stanley

Kissing the Hurt Away

"Mommy, my boo-boo hurts" you say earnestly –
Knowing Mommy will be able to bring much needed relief.

Mommy kisses the hurt and rubs it and asks, "Is it better?"

You smile,
      Say yes,
            Then go on your way…
                  Amazingly, all pain and troubles have gone away.

For the rest of your life Mommy will be here for your and glad to say
      "Tell me where it hurts, Baby,"
            And kiss the boo-boo away.

Peace on Earth

I've seen peace on earth
    To Mommy's joy and surprise
        The first time Daddy picked you up when you cried
            As you laid on his chest,
                The tears dried from your eyes!

The world at that moment was safe,
    Time stood still,
        Every day the peace grew stronger,
            Slowly and surely,
                As Daddy continued to dance his special dance to
                soothe your strong will.

What joy we have as your parents -
    We've been blessed with a precious gift of love…
        What joy to whisper secrets as you coo the night away
        We have the best daughter in the world -
            We've definitely been blessed that way!

Our whole world changed the day you arrived...
    I've seen peace on earth -
        And it is in your eyes!

© Eurydice Stanley

*Choose this day
whom you will serve...
...as for me and my house,
we will serve the Lord.*

Joshua 24:15

Interruption

Hello?

I'm playing with my baby...

Yes, that's her laughing...

Oh, you're making me miss something!

Please call back in 18 years after she leaves for college –

I'm sure I'll have some time for you then!

"Get a life?" - what do you mean?

This is the only life I've ever wanted!

We should definitely talk...

    later...

        much later...

            goodbye for now!

When I Knew You Were Mine
(Thank You Great-Grandma Rozelle)

Although I carried you for more than 10 months,
And felt your every move,
And watched you emerge from my stomach-
Large, beautiful, bigger than life, howling, and wailing-
Intensely upset at the doctors who lifted you from your warm,
comfortable cocoon…

And although I nursed you, at times completely numb from the pain of
    the C-section and the new experience of nursing…

It didn't seem I was officially your Mommy until Great-Grandma,
    Experienced Mother of 6,
        Life-long child caregiver and pleasant, congenial personality,
            Came to stay for awhile to help Mommy when Daddy
                had to go back to work.

She'd keep you during the day -
    Giving Mommy the chance to sleep,
        Having been up all night with you, colicky baby!

Each morning I'd hand you over-
    Exhausted from your screams throughout the night,
        You slept contentedly with no fuss in sight!

Mommy was filled with doubt,
    Becoming convinced that you'd be better cared for
        by such a "Mommy Master…"

But one morning…you didn't want to go…

You knew who your Mommy was –
    You knew my scent and my touch –
        You wanted to stay with me
            And you did.
                And Mommy wept.

I realized at that moment that although there may be better Mommy's,
There would always only be one "Grace's Mommy."

You chose me, and still do-
    I knew you were mine,
        And I have always known-
            I will always belong to you!

© Eurydice S. Stanley

76

What's Next?

What are you thinking, Busy Bee?

I see the wheels turning in your head!

Jump to the left – chew the remote control,

To the right the fish tank calls,

But don't forget tearing up Mom's work,

The greatest joy of all!

Shred the paper,

Hide the keys,

Pause to bring Daddy to his knees…

The work of a busy bee is never done!

I see you thinking –

Which task, Busy Bee, which one?

© Eurydice Stanley

*Charm is deceitful
and beauty is passing,
But a woman who
fears the Lord,
she shall be praised.*
Proverbs 31:30

Diva

The Princess is having a "Diva Moment" -
Fussing just because…
Crying her little eyes out,
Seemingly without love.

She demands attention NOW OR ELSE!
    Tribulation is sure to come!
        Watch out, she is no longer the sweet baby you once knew –
           Significant damage may soon be done!

What is it, Princess,
    That has caused you to fuss?
        And change your sweet demeanor to one that is cranky and
           gruff?

Where did that scowl come from?
    Don't mess up that pretty face! You can't always have your way -
        Mommy and Daddy will provide what's best for you each and
           every day!

Now, that's it -
    Give us that beautiful smile,
        Much better, Sunshine…
           Bring my Princess back, Diva,
               And let her stay awhile!

© Eurydice Stanley

Rest in the Lord.

Psalm 37:7

Yay, It's Naptime!

Yay, it's naptime!
  Mommy and Daddy get a break
    From the endless ripping and running
     A one year-old can make.

Yay, it's naptime!
  Mommy and Daddy jump with glee
    Time for your parents to regenerate
     In preparation for Round 3!

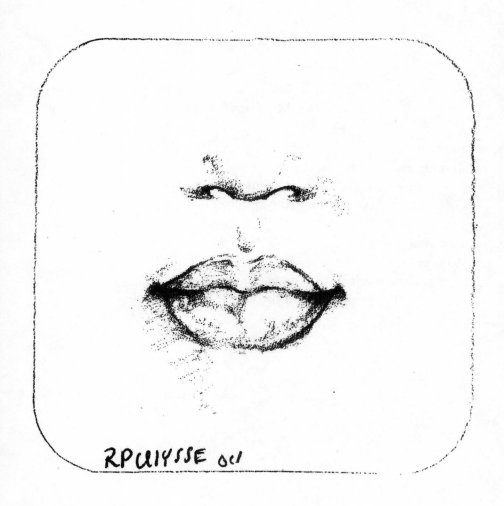

RPUIYSSE OU

Perfect Lips

Heart on the top,
Tinted in rose,
Bottom shaped like a half-moon crescent,
With a perfect button nose.

Soft, warm and tender
Are baby's sweet lips
Sharing kisses with Mommy and Daddy-
Ambrosia,
      Sweet nectar,
           Heaven sips!

© Eurydice Stanley

Manicures and Pedicures

(For Aunt Vanessa and the Girls)

What fun we have on "Salon Day"
Initiated whenever you say,
"More, Mommy" holding up a bottle of nail polish,
Wiggling your fingers and toes expectantly.

You sit very still as the polish is applied
And blow with all your might -
When your nails are dry you say "pretty"
And rush to show Daddy your shiny nails in the light!

© Eurydice Stanley

Where's My Camera?
(For Paw-Paw)

Where's my camera?
I know that it's here someplace!
Look at my baby's beautiful face!

Yes, I know we already have boxes of pictures galore,
But surely we could stand just one more!

Hold that look, Sweetie,
Let Mommy capture that smile,
I know you're only little for a short while!

Oh your outfit is so cute
And your hair a delight,
Just one more picture –
I promise, the last one tonight!

Tomorrow there are new outfits and adventures in store,
So I really can't say I won't take anymore…

You're cute as a button and sweet as a pea,
I can't help it - one more shot, please?
Go ahead, Princess,
Smile for Mommy!

© Eurydice Stanley

*Not that I speak
in respect of want:
for I have learned,
in whatsoever state I am,
therewith to be content.*

Philippians 4:11

You're More Than Enough
(Written before we were blessed with Christian!)

God's Grace is sufficient,
We don't need more,
But who is to tell what future blessings are in store?

We are so thankful for you, my Sweet,
And praise God everyday –
But we'll gladly welcome a brother or sister along the way!

Our Trinity of love can expand and grow,
There is room in our hearts for additions, we know!

With each new bundle of joy our capacity to love will expand -
There will never be limits to our hearts…
      although there may be limits to our hands…

But until that time, until that day,
God's Grace is sufficient in everyway!

© Eurydice Stanley

And she shall bring forth a Son, and thou shalt call His name Jesus: for He shall save His people from their sins.

Matthew 1:21

A Christmas to Remember
(Baby's First Christmas)

Like Baby Jesus you were given three gifts at Christmas…
    You opened them casually,
        but your interest was held *completely* by the packaging —
            The *boxes* were your true treat,
                with wrapping paper to tear and popcorn
                    to squeeze and eat!

You had hours of fun, Mommy and Daddy did too,
    The actual gifts weren't the issue - your joy was pure and true!

As you continued to play with the packaging, Dear,
    and tore paper with delight…
        Mommy gathered your gifts and put them away for the night.

The gifts were just a symbol, not important actually,
    They represented Jesus' sacrifice due to His love for you and me.

God's "true gifts" are most desired and can be enjoyed year-round,
    We're thankful for His holy "presents,"
        But His *Presence,* the Holy Spirit, is the greatest gift we've found!

Yes Angel, we had a Christmas to Remember -
    I'm glad Mommy and Daddy practiced restraint…
        We knew the reason for the season cannot found in meaningless
            Bobbles, toys and "stuff,"
                Rather, gratitude for Christ's birth
                And praise for our family's blessings -
                    We have more than enough!

God invites us to celebrate Jesus' birthday party each year -
    As His children, we're thankful for the celebration and so much more!
        We celebrate the significance of Christ's birth with praise,
            Knowing this wonderful celebration could not be represented
                by items from a store!

© Eurydice Stanley

Dance With Mommy

Come dance with Mommy, Sweetie-

Twirl, Ballerina –

Spin, Superstar –

Fly forever my love, fly!

Let Mommy's love lift you up beyond the sky!

As we waltz,

We smile,

We laugh,

We twirl…

Hear our music of love in your heart, forever -

You'll always be Mommy's girl!

© Eurydice Stanley

...He...fed thee
with manna,
which thou knewest not,
neither did thy fathers know;
that He might make thee
know that man not
live by bread only,
but by every word
that proceedeth out of
the mouth of the Lord
doth man live

Deuteronomy 8:3

Manna from Heaven

God provides milk from my breast to nourish the child He placed in my womb —
What a blessing!

Sustenance from heaven to strengthen a perfect little body,
What a miracle!

Cuddles from Mommy to soothe her soul,
Guidance from God to direct her life —
What joy!

Breastfed and nurtured -
Spirit-fed and strong —

What a well fed, well bred baby you are!

© Eurydice Stanley

Snuggling With Mommy
(Grace's favorite pastime while Mommy was pregnant)

Since you've discovered another baby is on the way,
You've attached yourself to Mommy,
Which is absolutely OK!

Since Mommy's energy is often spent after a day at work-
    We'll lay in bed and rest -
        Pressed close and snuggled tight,
            Whispering secrets and hugging all day and all night...

No, I don't have to worry that we're bonded –
It's often the opposite, you see,
Sometimes my big, sore, uncomfortable pregnant body just wants to say

      "GET OFF OF ME!"

But I realize our time is important –
    And it is critical for you to always know,
        That regardless of our new addition,
            You'll always be my baby – my firstborn!

You can feel free to snuggle with Mommy anytime, Princess,
    Even when you're grown!

© Eurydice Stanley

The Essence of My Baby

Sweetness beyond measure -
    Love complete.
        Beauty undefiled -
           Pretty toes and feet.

A head full of curly Q's,
    An inquisitive mind that cannot be quelled,
        A heart that knows no boundary -
           Kisses that make you melt!

The essence of my baby
    Is simple for all to see…
        My baby's exceptional essence
        Is love eternally!

© Eurydice Stanley

To everything
there is a season,
a time to every purpose
under heaven...
Ecclesiastes 3:1

Time to Wean the Baby

I've held you close to nourish you,
Now it is time to let go.
No more milk from Mommy – I'll prepare healthy food to help you grow.

It's so hard to stop breastfeeding you, Sweetie,
But stop I must-
So you're not over-reliant on Mommy,
Or use her as a "comfort crutch."

16 months should suffice,
And start you well on your way -
You've broken every height and weight chart at the doctor's office
And you continue to grow every day!

Please know that just because I've stopped nursing you, Baby,
It certainly does not mean
That Mommy will ever stop holding or loving you,
Simply because you've been weaned!

© Eurydice Stanley

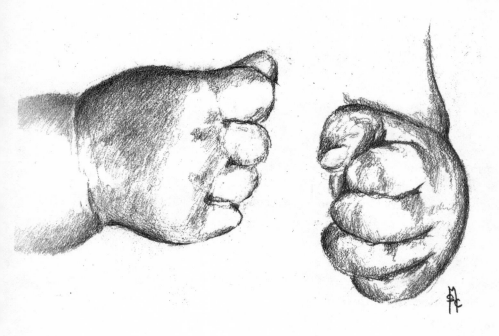

Captured Kisses
(For Ellen and Sweet Erin)

Hi sweet baby,
You look so precious lying there –
    Hands curled…
        Gnawing profusely on your fists…
          Toes wiggling…
            Big smile on your lips!

Could you do something for me?
    If you're not too busy, please…
        Hold my kiss in each hand,
          And from time to time, gently squeeze…

Thank you sweet baby –
    You'll see me all day and all through the night,
        But it makes me feel much better -
          Knowing my kisses are held tight!

© Eurydice S. Stanley

For this child I prayed;
and the Lord hath given me
my petition which
I asked of Him:
therefore also I have
lent him to the Lord;
as long as he liveth,
he shall be lent to the Lord...
1 Samuel 1:27–28

My Angel

Angel hair,

    Angel smile,

        Angel heart,

            Angel child…

                Loaned from Heaven up above –

                    Mommy's Sweet Angel of love!

                    © Eurydice Stanley

Adventures in Restauranting

Food goes in your mouth, not on the floor!

Please stop walking out the door!

Stop banging on the table with the fork and knife –

Must we stay home for the rest of our lives?

Please eat, Baby!

See, look, yum-yum!

I give up - let's share the pleasure of feeding you with Daddy,

Mommy shouldn't have all the fun!

© Eurydice Stanley

Mimic

The first time you were given your first "real" babydoll -

    You picked her up,

        And loved her,

            And kissed her,

                And placed her up on your shoulder,

                    And patted her back,

                        And sang to her…

                            Just like Mommy did with you!

*For whoever shall
do the will of my Father
which is in heaven
the same is my brother,
and sister, and mother.*

Matthew 12:50

Extended Family
(Too many Aunties and Uncles to list by name – we love you all!)

Give Uncle and Auntie a hug,

No, they are not your relatives by blood.

Actually, their tie is much stronger…you see,

They *chose* to love us,

They *chose* to care,

They *chose* to check in on us,

And they *chose* to always be there.

We're blessed to have them,

And they feel the same way too –

But most importantly, Dear,

There are more people in the world to guide and love you!

© Eurydice Stanley

New Teeth

Ouch!

Where did that come from?

Another tooth? Wow!

They seem to come everyday...

I really didn't envision teething this way...

Oh Sweetie, don't cry...

Mommy knows it hurts now and makes you sad,

Look at your pretty, pearly white smile –

Soon the pain won't be so bad!

© Eurydice Stanley

Who Are Godparents?
(For Godfather and Godmother Joe and God-Grandfather Nichols)

Should something happen to Mommy and Daddy,
    God made a special plan -

That caregivers aside from blood family
    would stand before Him and say,
        "I'll care for and love this child in every way."

They are God's "safety net," ensuring you always have
    Whatever it is your little heart desires
        or needs to make you happy and glad!

Lord willing, Mommy and Daddy will always be with you,
    But Godparents just guarantee,
        You'll always have wonderful, caring people to provide
      The love, guidance, and attention
          that a sweet baby like you needs!

© Eurydice Stanley

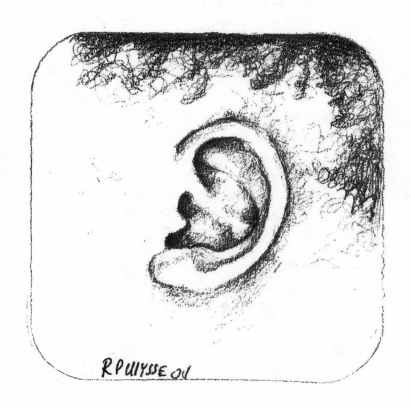

Stop It!

Stop it this minute!

    Do you hear me?

        I mean it…that is not cute!

Well, actually it is…but stop it!!

    Uh, keep going *only* until Daddy gets the video camera…

        But after that, you have to stop – for real!

Wait, hold it –

    That is a great shot right there –

        Mommy must take a picture…

            Just don't do it again next time, OK?

You are so silly…

    I can't help but laugh…

        Please stop…

            You're killing me…

            You're so cute…

                We took some great shots…

                Please stop…

                Please?

© Eurydice Stanley

...out of the strong
came forth Sweetness...
Judges 14:6

Brown Sugar

"Brown Sugar Baby,"

    Your kisses taste so good,

        and you're so good to me!

Natural,

    Sweet,

        Granulated or hard-packed,

            You melt in extreme heat, so I must handle with care...

You dissolve within your surroundings,

    Making them better,

        More flavorful,

            And much more satisfying!

Brown Sugar, you're a natural complement to anything you touch -

    Making it complete,

        Tasty,

            Tantalizing,

                And desired very much!

Sweet Brown Sugar Baby, you're so good!

Unto the pure
all things are pure...
Titus 1:5

Amazing

You are simply amazing…every part of you…from head to toe.

Each day is a new adventure,

A new accomplishment,

A new day of just being *you*,

Pure, real and sweet;

Truly a wonderful blessing to me –

You're simply amazing!

© Eurydice Stanley

Lo, children are an heritage of the Lord: and the fruit of the womb

Psalm 127:3

Heritage of Love
(For Grandma (Priscilla), Great-Grandma Mitchell and Great-Grandma Rozelle)

People ask "How is it that you speak of your baby with such love and esteem?"

Mommy always wonders, "What do you mean?"

You see-

Mommy heard these words from her Mommy and Grandmas as a little girl,
　　She was often told she was the best in the whole wide world!

So it is quite natural (and true) for Mommy to say
　　Words of love and encouragement to you each day.

Mommy knows you're brilliant, bold, without boundary and beautiful, it's true...
　　Succeed or fail, Princess, your family will always love you!

There is nothing you can't do,
　　And nothing from which you'd be discouraged (unless it was harmful for you).

"Go get 'em Tiger,"
　　You'll go far-
　　　　　　Your family is completely behind you, Honey,
　　　　　　　　Go out and be the winner that you are!

What Are You Doing?

You've got one leg up on the table and another in the air,

    As you munch on a cookie and talk to someone who isn't there.

If only I could experience such contentment and happiness galore,

    But actually I do, -

        through you -

            ever-wondering what next you have in store!

            © Eurydice Stanley

"Gifts In My Glass"
(Also Known As Backwash!)

No, you have to drink from your cup –

Mommy's is the same,

But hers doesn't have dinner floating in it –

Too many things to name!

No, this is not for baby!

Oh no, you grabbed it anyhow!

Mommy will get another glass – you can have it now!

© Eurydice Stanley

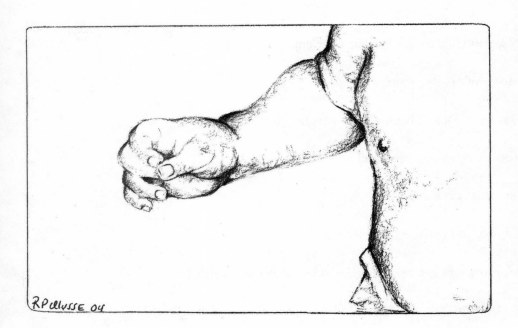

RPalusse 04

118

You Are Perfect for Nibbling!

Oh how big, sweet and juicy you are!

Dimpled elbows,
Dimpled knees,
Big round tummy -
Chubby cheeks!

Toes made for chewing,
Thunder thighs,
I know a neck is in there somewhere-
Between your shoulders and your eyes!

Mommy's big baby -
Tall, stocky and strong…
Mommy could nibble and kiss on you all day long!

© Eurydice Stanley

A Warning to the Babysitter…
(Should we ever actually get one)

I'm entrusting you with my most precious gift -
Please handle with care.
I'm entrusting you with my reason for living –
Please watch her as if I were here.

I'm warning you now,
    She's quick as a whip - it really doesn't take long…
        She's very creative and exceptionally smart-
            It's not hard for her to find something
                where she doesn't belong!

She may not want to eat,
    And may resist sleep,
        Just like any other kid,
            But that is where the similarities cease-
                She's more intelligent and loving than most –
                Soon you'll see as I did!

She's a very good baby
    And for the most part, she'll do as she's told –
        Just play with her,
            Read to her,
              Talk to her,
                Stimulate her mind and remember,
                Her heart is pure gold!

I realize accidents can happen
But please make sure,
The television is not used as a caregiver
And you're watching her as if she were yours.

One last thing –
Please believe it's true…
Should anything happen to my child due to your neglect –
May Heaven help you!

© Eurydice Stanley

Big Hug!
(Dedicated to Uncles Que-Que and Aaron)

Oh, that was the BIGGEST hug in the whole wide world!

How sweet you are – and strong!

I'm locked up in your pudgy arms surrounded by love –

It's hard to believe your chunky legs squeezing my waist are so long!

You SQUEEZE with all your might,

Then pat my back comfortingly - pure delight!

What a hug from Heaven!

Could it be?

Yes, the bonus of a sweet kiss –

Nothing else could possibly make me as happy!

Another Big Hug!

Ok, I promise, last one for the night…

Alright, just one more…this could go on until daylight!

© Eurydice Stanley

But my God shall supply all your needs according to His riches in glory by Christ Jesus.

Philippians 4:19

I Promise
(For Mommy's Babies, With True Love...)

I promise...

    I will love you forever,

        I will speak life into you,

            I will treat you with respect,

                I will support you,

                    I will be silly with you,

                        I will cry with you,

                            I would die for you,

                              I promise –

                                Always.

War May Call

(Dedicated to all Servicewomen and Men)

Mommy may have to go away for awhile
Because of something called war…

It is not that Mommy doesn't love you or wants to leave you,
But there are some things worth fighting for…

I know it is hard to understand, Sweetie, but this is something I must do!

Daddy will be here to love, watch and care for you while I'm gone –
I know you'll be in wonderful hands, Honey, be strong!

Believe when Daddy tucks you in at night, Mommy will be right there…
Pray for Mommy until she returns to give you tender loving care!

I can't say there won't be tears while I'm away,
Because I'll miss my sweet Angel every single day!

The tears you cry,
    I'll cry as well, this you must know!
        I'd give almost anything for the privilege of watching you grow –
           …that privilege, called freedom, is precisely why I must go!

Freedom is not free, Dear, nor will it ever be,
Many others have paid a price much more than Mommy's.

Daddy will tell me all of your quests
But know that in my mind's eye I'll see your adventures and ask you to rest!

I'll see you smile,
    I'll watch you walk,
        I'll hear you anxiously try to talk.
           I'll feel your arms wrap around my neck,
              And even feel the comfort of you patting my back.

When I return we'll pick up where we started,
Until then, Dearheart, let's not be brokenhearted!

I will be here with you, if only in your heart and mind,
    Love me, Dear, as I will you, until the end of time!

Should war call, keep me close in your heart, Sweetie, as I will you,
    Be a good girl for Daddy…I promise, I'll always love you!
        With God's Grace, Angel, I'll see you soon!

© Eurydice Stanley

O taste and see that the Lord is good

Psalm 34:8

"Ambrosia"

Sweet Baby,
    You are a decadent pleasure,
        Simply delicious!

I look at you and see a sumptuous feast of happiness, peace, joy,
    faith and a future of hope.

I indulge in your endless bounty daily,
    Yet I'm never satiated...
        I always want more-
            But no more than you can give, my Dear.

Tasty Treat,
    You're so good to me...and FOR me...

No calories,

No guilt,
    Except occasional sadness for those who do not have the
        opportunity for such precious communion daily...

Savory snack,
    Your wonderful banquet of delight guarantees Mommy will
        keep returning for more!

© Eurydice Stanley

Happy Easter, Sunshine!

Time to rise, Sunshine –
As Jesus did this day,
When others sought Him they found the tombstone had been rolled away!

Today we celebrate Jesus' Resurrection-
And do this most thankfully,

Because of His sacrifice our sins are forgiven-
Believers are set free!

So as you partake of the days' festivities, Sweetie,
Never forget the sacrifice that was made for you long ago…
Jesus walked the earth, gave His life and rose again because He loves you so!

© Eurydice Stanley

Happily Snowed In
(Hunkered down with baby during a Virginia blizzard)

It is early in the morning,
There is snow and ice outside,
We cuddle by the fireplace,
Under a soft, fuzzy blanket we hide.

No agenda –
We snuggle,
Mommy tickles a few secret spots,
You nurse and sneak a snack,
Mommy steals a few kisses,
We both laugh.

Me and my baby,
My baby and me,
No closer to perfection could a moment be!

Please don't get up!
Let Mommy have this time…
I'll have to let go soon enough…

But not now…

Not today…

Not this morning…

Not for a long while…

For now and forever –
It's just Me and my Baby,
My Baby and Me…
No closer to perfection could a wonderful snowy day be!

© Eurydice Stanley

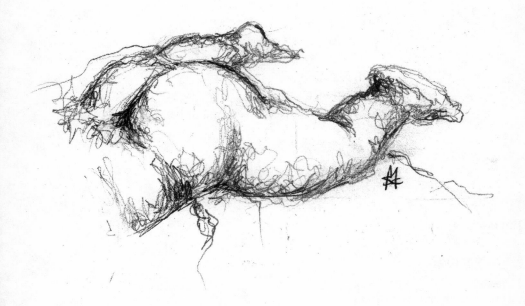

A Visit to the Doctor

Another trip to the Doctor-
    Lord, help me please!
        I know my baby is fine,
            But the thought of anything going wrong
                brings me to my knees!

Really, the check-ups aren't so bad…
    I like the height and weight charts
        (they confirm you've grown so big and strong!),
            But it's the painful immunization shots I can't take –
            I'd rather send your Dad!

When you cry, so do I-
    When you're sick, I really don't trust what the Doctor says…
        A second opinion wouldn't hurt, would it?

I'm a new Mommy…
    I know they expect my responses and I comply as if on cue…
        I consider my job important and I have nothing else to do
            But ensure the best and proper care is afforded you!

Thank goodness,
    I've got a few month's reprieve before we have to do this again…
        I need the time to build my confidence
            Maybe it would help if I bring a friend?

Perhaps I could convince Daddy to take you instead next time?
    I'm sure that would alleviate a lot of stress…
        Who am I kidding? I have to be there…
            When it comes to Baby care – Mommy knows best!

© Eurydice Stanley

Her children arise up,
and call her blessed;
her husband also,
and he praiseth her.

Proverbs 31:28

My Mother's Day Gift

On the day of your birth I was given a precious gift-
    The privilege to be called "Mommy" by the sweetest child on earth!

You're an answer to fervent prayer
    I knew one day you'd be mine,
        But the reality of you is so much better than the dream –
        I'll love you until the end of time!

Dear Baby,
    While I appreciate the gifts you have given me this day,
        Know that my true gift is *you* –
        In every possible way!

© Eurydice Stanley

And God shall wipe
away all tears from
their eyes; and there
shall be no more death,
neither sorrow
nor crying,
neither shall there
be anymore pain:
for the former things
are passed away.

Revelation 21:4

Colic Blues
(Why Are You Crying?!?)

Why are you crying?
    There is nothing wrong!
        Those tears aren't authentic –
            You've been fussy all day long!

I've fed you,
    Burped you,
        Rocked you,
            Changed you,
                Nursed you,
                    Played with you,
                        Sang to you,
                            And did everything I knew to do!

So why are you crying?
    Please stop, Baby Sweet!
        Your cries make Mommy's nerves scattered and brings her to tears –
        Not to mention causing constant ringing in her ears!

...the Lord seeth not as man seeth; for man looketh on the outward appearance, but the Lord looketh on the heart.

1 Samuel 16:7

Heartbeat

All is quiet in the house,
    Everyone is asleep,
        I stand by your bed smiling to myself,
            Cherishing the magic sound of your heartbeat.

How wonderful you are, Baby —
    A miracle to be sure-
        Each beat brings us closer...
            Mommy's Baby, Mommy's Girl!

© Eurydice Stanley

Happy Birthday, Sweetheart!

Happy Birthday, Sweetheart!
Where did the time fly?
365 days gone seemingly in the blink of an eye!

Look at you! Such a big girl!
You've grown and matured –
What happened to Mommy's baby, Mommy's little girl?

©Eurydice Stanley

*Fulfill ye my joy,
that ye be likeminded,
having the same love,
being of one accord,
of one mind.*
Philippians 2:2

"The Oneness"

You represent "The Oneness" of us-
    The love of your parents,
        And the love Christ has for His Church.

You represent the best of us-
    All that is good-
        Removing our flaws and what is not as desired
          But forgiven -
            Due to Christ's sacrifice.

What a perfect circle of love we represent –

    God loves Daddy loves Mommy loves Baby loves God loves Mommy
    loves Daddy loves Baby loves God...

God...

  Daddy...

    Mommy...

      Baby...

        Everything begins and ends with God's sacrificial love –

      We are One...Eternally.

© Eurydice Stanley

The righteous eats
to the Satisfying
of his soul
Proverbs 13:22

Baby Sandwich!

When I get hungry and feel empty inside,

It is not behind food that I try to hide…

Instead I hurry home for the nourishment I need-
I'll grab a "Baby Sandwich" and be satisfied, indeed!

The ingredients are simple, but healthy for sure…
Lay a sweet baby on top of a loafing Mommy –

     Cuddle,
          Giggle,
               Kiss,
                    Laugh,
                        Repeat!

Baby Sandwich – yummy and completely satisfying – my favorite treat!

© Eurydice Stanley

*I, even I am He
who comforts you...*
Isaiah 51:12

Cry

Now why would you mess up that face with tears,
     Wrinkling up your forehead, nose and ears?

Why turn red from fussing, stress and strain,
     And cause your parents unnecessary pain?

Hush, Sweet Baby,
     Soothe your soul,

Breathe, I promise it will be OK...
     Save your current angst for grown-up problems another day!

© Eurydice Stanley

The Daddy-Daughter Connection

There is no denying the special bond between Mommy & Daughter from birth,
  But the "Daddy-Daughter Connection" is also special –
    It helps a little girl identify love, values, her beauty and self-worth.

This connection is important, Sweetie,
  From Daddy you'll see,
    How you should be properly treated by a man,
      And what true love can be.

Your Daddy is so gentle with you
  Anticipating every perceived need,
    So should your future husband –
      Settle for nothing less, and always let God lead!

© Eurydice Stanley

*You have made known
to me the ways of life;
You will make me
full of joy
in your presence*

Acts 2:28

Baby Fulfillment

You fortify us –

    You sustain us –

        You motivate us –

            You ground us –

                You make us whole…

Thank you for loving us…We love you too!

    You give us purpose –

        You center us –

            You make the world make sense…

                You represent complete satisfaction in one small,

                    Perfect package!

© Eurydice Stanley

For He shall give His angels charge over thee, to keep thee in all thy ways.

Psalm 91:11

You're Incredible!

You're incredible!

How did you do that?

You're amazing!

Who taught you how to do that?

    It wasn't Daddy...

        It wasn't Mommy...

           How did you know?

It must have been the Angels that provide counsel wherever you go!

© Eurydice Stanley

No!

I know you want what you want ,
    and you're used to getting your way,
        But stop it, little girl, I mean it-
           Listen to what Mommy has to say!

You can't always have what you want when you want it,
    And often it is for your own good,
        Please don't see this as negative, Honey –
           I want to be understood!

Mommy and Daddy are here to protect you,
    And help you find your way,
        So if we tell you "No"
           Believe us, you may get hurt if you continue to roughly play!

So stick in that lip, Sweetie,
    Quiet down, stop those tears –
        Mommy and Daddy will continue tell you no
           To ensure you're here safely for years and years!

© Eurydice Stanley

As It Should Be
(For Pastor and Co-Pastor Dukes)

We love you Honey, but let's be clear -
Our first focus must be Jesus,
    Then one another,
        and then you, my Dear!

This order is madated by God, and keeps the family in sync,
    If we follow His perfect plan for our lives
        We will always have a strong link.

The Bible says Daddy must love Mommy as Christ loves His church -
    More than himself (after God), he must put her first...
        She is to be his glory and he must treat her as such,
            He must cherish her, or he does not love himself very much!

Mommy is expected to follow Daddy as Daddy follows Christ,
    This is not a burden, Honey,
        God is the ruler of our lives!
            He wants the best for us and provides daily as we pray,
                So Mommy trusts God to lead Daddy in the right way.

As much as Mommy and Daddy speak of their love for you,
    We know that God must come first as He leads and guides us to be
        Better people, better spouses
        And the best Daddy and Mommy!

So don't be upset by our focus, Sweetie,
    You are our sunshine to be sure -
        But we must love one another and focus on Jesus, our *Sonshine*,
        Through love for Him and each other,
            Mommy and Daddy can love you more!

© Eurydice Stanley

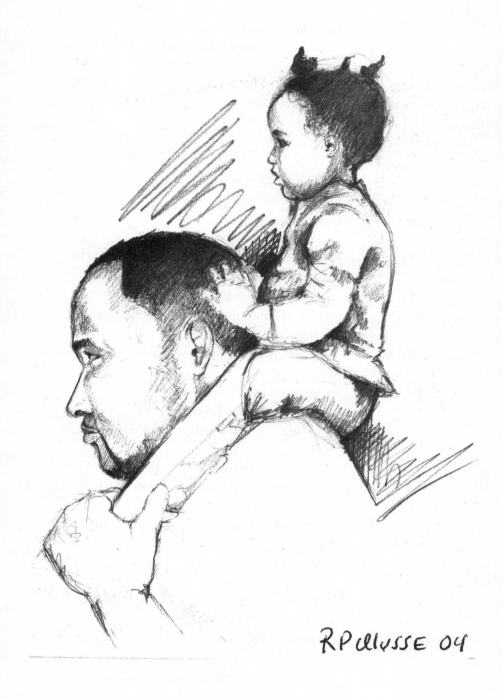

RPallusse 04

Daddy's Girl, Mommy's Baby

Daddy lets you have your way,

He's your personal jungle-gym for play.

You squeal with joy should he come near, but if you shed a tear...

It's Mommy you want,

Mommy you call,

Mommy you reach for,

Especially should you fall.

Yes, you're God's child –

Daddy's girl,

And Mommy's baby,

The best of all possible worlds,

For one special little lady!

© Eurydice Stanley

What a Performance!

Oh My – What a Performance!
        Best Actress quality!
                You'll definitely receive an Oscar or two –

Your rendition is quite compelling,
        I'd almost believe your trauma is true…

Except -

        I know you're fed,
        I know you're dry,
        No one has bothered you,
        We both know why you cry…

You've figured out that a little pout can go a long way –
        If Mommy won't react, Daddy will –

Yes, you've wrapped us around your little baby finger in the past,
        But now we're consciously fighting your spell –

Screaming and crying won't gain attention -
        Being a good, sweet baby will!

© Eurydice Stanley

Where Are You Going Busy Bee?
(For Auntie Sue and Cousin C1!)

Where are you going Busy Bee?

Why won't you come and sit with me?

Life will soon fill your days with **unimportant chores,**

And people will try to convince you **their job is yours!**

Don't be fooled, my Darling...

Remember to stop and smell the roses -

Breathe deeply, my Sweet,

Know that Living, not *Doing* makes life complete!

© Eurydice Stanley

Wonderful!

One Saturday morning,

Not long after you turned 2,

You sat on my lap watching cartoons and I played with
your hair absent-mindedly...

I said (as usual) "I love you, Baby."

You normally respond similarly,

But not this morning...Instead, you turned matter-of-factly and said

"Thank you, Momma," and continued watching cartoons...

And I melted from the intensity of my love for you,

Marveled at your depth...

And basked in the glow of your sweetness.

© Eurydice S. Stanley

Life-Long Friends
The Challenge of a Military Child
(For Ashanti, Camille, David Michael, Manuel, Isaac, Janae, Xochtil, Chloe,
Cole, and Logan!)

Military life can be hard, Sweetie, I'm sorry we have to go…
I know you don't want to leave your friends,
But just remember true friendship is not based on nearness -
It never really ends.

So even though you won't see your friends daily anymore,
It doesn't mean they're gone from our hearts and minds -
It just means we'll cherish letters, calls and visits more,
We'll communicate our love in any way we can find!

So for now, we'll have one last puppet show,
Watch a video and play tag,
Try not to cry, Honey, please try not to be sad!

You'll meet new friends wherever we go
Then you'll also have the old with the new -
More friends to grow, play, laugh, and learn with
And love you too!

© Eurydice Stanley

*Many daughters
have done virtuously,
but thou
excellest them all.*

Proverbs 31:29

Learning Through You
(For Uncle Thumper and Aunt Netta)

So many lessons to learn, baby –
The opportunity to see things brand-new,
I thank God for the chance to grow and develop through you!

Lessons range from the nonsensical –
    (Why do I know all your favorite TV characters by name?)

To the whimsical –
    (Princess colors are pink, lavender and gold…)

From the practical –
    (Never give a baby chili beans)

To the life-changing-
    (You're a model of unconditional love – you smile never grows old!)

Every moment you share an exciting gem that I hold in my heart –
With you I'll be a life-long learner – each day is a brand-new start!

© Eurydice Stanley

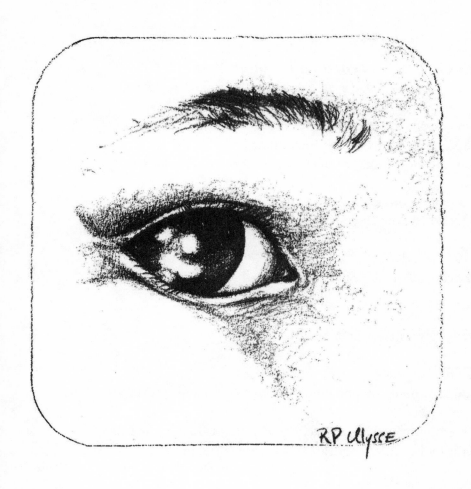

RP Ulysse

Through a Daughter's Eyes
(For My Mommy, Priscilla)

When I was a little girl,
I used to watch and stare,
As my Mommy prepared for her workday,
Combing through her long, beautiful, flowing hair.

I remember the stocking-clad curve of her calf,
And the shine of her gloss applied lips,
The shadow complimenting her eyes,
And the suit complimenting her hips.

I thought, "My Mommy is the prettiest woman in the whole world" -
She definitely was to me,
And when people said I looked like her,
I'd smile with pride and glee.

Now I have my own wonderful daughter,
And from the corner of my eye,
I often catch her staring,
As I comb my hair and my make-up is applied.

I often wonder what she is thinking,
And hope one day she'll see,
Her daughter looking up at her,
Recognizing the beauty (inside and out) of her Mommy.

© Eurydice Stanley

Mommy's Life Force
(Smile Uncle Bobby!)

When conflicts arise at work,
I fervently pray to the Lord - I beg, I plea!
   "Father, please remove this person
      who's sucking the life force out of me!"

He often provides serenity and escape, however,
   By letting my mind soar
      To my Sweet Baby Girl who at the end of the day
       will be waiting for me by the door.

Thoughts of her always provide infused strength,
   And my patience begins to return –
      Rather than being depleted by the offending party,
       through my child, I am restored!

As I think of my Baby and what really counts
   Due to her sweetness and Christ's intervention I am able to say,
    "One moment please- let's start over - How can I help you today?"

© Eurydice Stanley

Store "Investigations"...Stay With Mommy!

Busy Bee,
I know you think it's important to conduct a reconnaissance of
       everything in a store you see,
           But Sweetie, I implore you – stay with Mommy!

When you slip away to investigate wonders unseen,
My heart stops during those seconds until you're found,
I'm upset, I'm scared – my breathing is bound!

Unfortunately this world is not safe, Sweetie -
Not everyone has your best interests at heart,
Mommy knows this all too well and asks you to please do your part!

I know the Lord has His hand on you,
And I trust Him to keep you in His care,
I also take seriously the responsibility of keeping you safe from harm
       while you're here on earth -
But I know that with your every step, Angels are always there!

I promise, Sweetie, together we'll go and see
Every secret place of interest to you, Busy Bee.
Just stay with Mommy, Honey -
       With the Lord's help I'll ensure you're safe and protected,
          Not unsupervised in a world where you could be hurt,
            harmed or neglected!

© Eurydice Stanley

*Pleasant words are
as an honeycomb,
sweet to the soul
and health to the bones.*

Proverbs 16:24

Every Day is Sweeter

Every day with you is sweeter than the day before,
Although I didn't think it possible, with each day I love you more!

Each morning I awake and wonder, what incredible thing will the baby
      do today?
Then I thank the Lord for the privilege of allowing me to watch you
      learn, grow and play.

Today was wonderful, Sweetie, but really, Mommy can't wait,
      To welcome the joys tomorrow will bring –
            I know our life together will continue to be great!

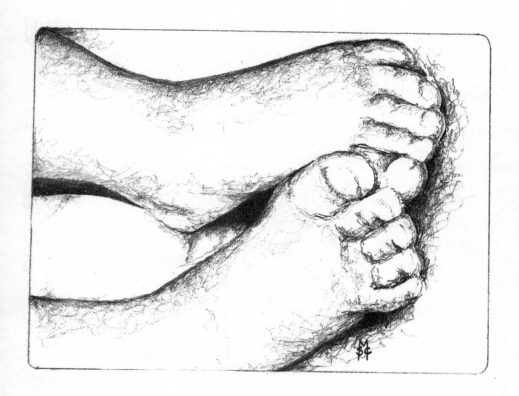

Great Parts Make a Great Whole!

Dimpled elbows,
Dimpled knees,
Rolls of thighs,
Bulging belly to tickle, fill and please.

Fingertips with prints,
Unique to only you,
Toesies for chewing,
A heart that is pure in all you do.

All these wonderful parts
Create a breathtaking, magnificent whole!
We're blessed with the best baby in the nation,
A perfect example of God's creation!

© Eurydice Stanley

Strong Sense of Ownership
(Thank you for your patience, NanaTiti Rachel!)

My cup!

My baby!

My toy!

My book!

How can everything be yours upon the first look?

My blankie!

My bear!

My milk!

My phone!

Is there anything that is not yours alone?

But admittedly, I beam with pride when you say "MY MOMMY" to
      Newcomers,
           Bystanders,
                Perceived threats,
                      Or even people on the phone –

Yes Angel, you're right – *your Mommy alone!*

© Eurydice Stanley

Grace Is Mommy's Baby
(A silly song the baby enjoys)

Grace is Mommy's Baby,
Don't say maybe!
Grace is Mommy's Baby,
Baby girl!
Baby girl!

© Eurydice Stanley

Behold, how good
and how pleasant it is
for brethren to dwell
together in unity!

Psalm 133:1

Mommy's Home!

Hello Bright Eyes!

    It is so good to see you!

I thought about you all day –

    Did you notice I was gone, or think of me too?

Yes, I can see from your delighted response that you share my glee –

    You jump, reach up and your bright eyes say

        "Mommy, play with me!"

Tell me, Sweetie, how was your day?

    Tell me, what did you do? What did you say?

We've got all evening to catch up, although the hours are too few…

    Regardless, Mommy is glad to see you!

        It is good so to see your love and light;

            You're a wonderful welcome home, Bright Eyes -

            We'll have a beautiful night!

© Eurydice Stanley

Daycare Drama

Mommy has to go to work now and you have to stay –

Please, please Honey, please don't look at me that way!

It is hard enough to leave you –
    Mommy is filled with guilt and doubt-
        But it is that much worse at the daycare when you fall out!

I know you want to stay with Mommy, but she has to go to work,
    Please stop crying, convulsing, and making your body jerk!

Each time this happens I'm a wreck for the rest of the day –
    I drive to work in tears and frazzled,
        Constantly trying to think of another way!

You know that I'd keep you if I possibly could,
    Believe Mommy, Honey, this is for your own good!

Please don't cry, Honey, it is something Mommy can't take –
    Please stop or I'm sure Mommy's heart will break!

Just 8 hours, Baby, I promise, then I'm through…
    Mommy will soon be back to take care of you!

Your sitter was especially selected to care just for you –
    She'll love and protect you until Mommy is through!

I have to go now…have a good time playing, Sweetie,
    PLEASE look like you'll have fun!
        If you don't, Mommy will cry incessantly until her day is done!

© Eurydice Stanley

Perfect Proportions

Big Tummy,

Pudgy knees,

Soft Toes,

Round Cheeks.

Gigantic heart,

My big ball of love -

Extraordinary proportions in such a small package –

A gift from God above!

Trinity of Love

Father,
Son,
Holy Ghost -

Daddy,
Mommy,
Baby.

Trinity of Love,
      Trinity of Commitment,
            Trinity of Responsibility,
                  Trinity of Sacrifice,
                        Trinity of Praise!

Thank you, Father God for triune love
      And the strength that lies therein;
            Our unified home creates a harbor of safety for the family,
            A place where peace lies within.

© Eurydice Stanley

Cooties Galore

(For Dr. Jude and Dr. Soberano - Thanks for the excellent care!)

I know you have to go to daycare
But I really cannot take,
The cooties you're exposed to daily –
It seems we never get a break!

Antibiotics again?
Too many brands to name –
I wish I knew who gave you this sickness - who is to blame?

The medicine's side effects can be just as bad
As the prescriptions you take -
From diarrhea to vomiting - I'm confused, tell me nurse,
Are we fixing the problem or making it worse?

Doctor, I know you're here to help and being careful,
But am I supposed to be glad we came
As my baby cries and continues to call out my name?

If it is not a virus, it's a cold, with all the usual signs-
    Runny nose,
        Watery eyes,
            Loss of appetite – AAAHHH - Oh my!
All Mommy can do is pray, love and care for you and sigh!

Finally!
You're back to health!
Off to school you go!
Oh no – look at all these runny noses in your class…
Cootie Alert!
Touch nothing, Sweetie, until you come home!

© Eurydice Stanley

Grace Is...

(Another nonsensical sing-along-song my baby enjoys)

Grace is the sweetest girl in the world
Grace is the nicest girl in the world
Grace is the smartest girl in the world,

Yes she is!
Yes she is!

And I know-
I know because her Mommy said so,
And everything her Mommy says,
About that baby is true -
That's why I say...
That everything is A-OK,
And anytime Grace wants to play,
That's when her Mommy will come play!

Because...

Grace is the sweetest girl in the world,
Grace is the nicest girl in the world,
Grace is the smartest girl in the world,

Yes she is!
Yes she is!

© Eurydice Stanley

Liquefied Dinner

You will sit with mashed potatoes in your mouth

Until they turn to runny soup-

Ground beef becomes liquid puree',

And bread becomes paste…

Why do you do this?!?

We can't let this food go to waste!

You will eat or sit in time-out-

The choice is yours, my Dear,

You need the nutrition to grow big and strong –

Taking God's bounty for granted is not a luxury that will last long!

I know you don't yet understand the things that I say,

But just trust Mommy, Honey –

Eat up!

You're blessed - God willing, you'll stay that way!

© Eurydice Stanley

Family Fun Day!

(Dedicated to my family, who make lounging an art!)

Sometimes work gets too hectic,
And what's most important isn't clear –

So when Mommy needs to refocus her energy and find her way,
She'll shout out to everyone – "It's Family Fun Day!"

We don't have to go anywhere,
Actually, being at home is best –

Providing the opportunity to relax and snuggle together,
And get some much needed rest!

Hugs and kisses are central aspects of the day -
Laughter, tickling and giggling galore –

Eating many comfort foods is key,
And, of course, we'll rest up some more!

Laying together, we may watch a movie -
Happily we'll all laugh and look,

Regardless of what we do, we do it *together*,
From making dinner to reading a book!

Family Fun Day is great!
Cherished time for our "team" –

Thank you God for an outlet
That helps us rejuvenate, revive and beam!

© Eurydice Stanley

181

Accomplishment

When I pick you up from pre-school, I ask "What did you do today, Princess?"

Each day without fail you smile and excitedly respond –

"I go potty!" (All by yourself? Big Girl!)

"I wash hands!" (Your hands are clean? Let Mommy see...very good!)

I marvel at your sense of accomplishment,

And almost envy your pride...

Wishing I could be as happy about my day...

I can't think of anything that could be considered as important –

Nothing compares!

Conversely,

Burdens from the day are lessened, as well –

My baby went potty by herself!

Who cares about that horrible meeting!

She washed her hands!

Problems faced today will eventually be resolved...

Princess, you're wonderful...

Thanks for putting life in perspective!

© Eurydice Stanley

Miss Independence
(Thank you Miss Mary, Diane and Sarah)

As I drive you to daycare I brace for the worst…

But today,

    You run in to class,

        Say hi to your teacher,

            Show her your baby,

                Then turn to me and say "Bye, Mommy…"

                    And I stare with my jaw open in disbelief.

As I stand there,

    You turn back to me as if to say

        "You're still here?

            I promptly leave happily -

            And I love it!

© Eurydice Stanley

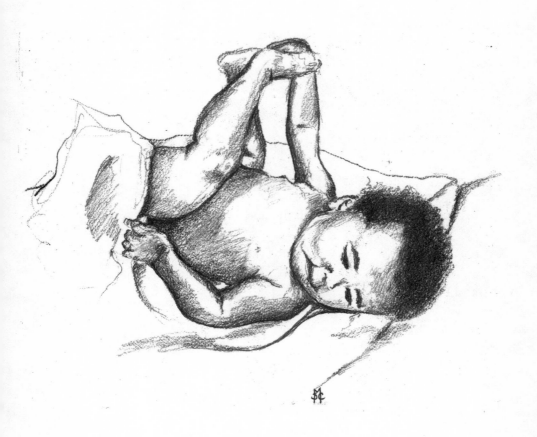

Thank You, Father

(Grace's Lyric)

Thank you Father, for my blessing
Thank you for this babe,
Thanks for showing your love through me,
In Jesus' holy name.

Build up this weak vessel,
Strengthen this temple true,
Create in me a clean heart,
Reflecting the love of You.

Thank you Father, for my blessing
Thank you for this babe,
Thanks for showing your love through me,
In Jesus' holy name.

Thank you for this Sunshine,
Reflecting the love of your Son,
Let her be a ray of hope,
Continuing the work you've begun.

Thank you Father, for my blessing
Thank you for this babe,
Thanks for showing your love through me,
In Jesus' holy name!

© Eurydice Stanley

*And if ye be Christ's,
then are ye
Abraham's Seed,
and heirs accordingly
to the promise.*
Galatians 3:29

Your Greatness Has Been Prophesied
(For All the World's Children - Grow in God's Greatness!)

You are Abraham's seed called of God –
You have a priceless inheritance as His child!

The Lord called you by name before you were born -
Follow His guidance, fulfill your destiny and receive His eternal reward.

Stay in your Word and know it's true,
      The gifts and ministries of others can be yours too -
           God's opportunities are limitless for you!

God promised with His Strength that you can do All Things -
With Him, Dear Child and you can be ABSOLUTELY ANYTHING:

      Wiser than Solomon,
      Braver than Esther,
      A survivor of great adversity like Joseph,
      An obedient visionary like Noah,
      With more discernment than Deborah...
      You can be an exceptional communicator like Aaron,
      A great leader like Moses,
      Stronger than Samson,
      Tenacious like Jacob,
      With the prophecy of Jeremiah...
      You can show exceptional devotion like Ruth,
      Be an insightful teacher like Paul,
      With a servant's heart like Martha...

You are the Lord's beautiful, glorious wonders -
      Always remember you are beloved of God like David;
           Have the humility of John the Baptist
               And the worship intimacy of Mary...

You are Spiritual Warriors created with love -
      Blessed by grace,
           Wrapped in affection,
               Approved and self-assured,
                  Anointed by God -
                    Loved by All!

*For ye are all
the children of God
by faith in
Christ Jesus*

Galatians 3:26

Should Anything Ever Happen
(For Grace and Christian, My Beloved Babies)

Should anything ever happen
     And Mommy is no longer here,
          You must know in your hearts cherished cherubs
               How much I will always love you - even if I am not near.

If Mommy is called home to Heaven
     Before you come of age,
          Know I will continue to care for you from up above
          And watch over you every minute of the day.

I would never leave you of my own will, Babies,
     But we must trust God's perfect plan-
          Rely on Jesus as you do now, let Him guide your steps -
          He will lead you to the Promised Land!

Just as God is with you always,
     Mommy will be there too -
          You'll see me in the daily little things you see and do...

When you sit, know you're on Mommy's lap,
     And I'm wrapping my arms around you tight;
          The sunshine will be my smile of pride -
          You'll always be my source of true delight!
          Rain will be Mommy's tears,
               As I will very much miss you too; but take comfort,
                   After every rain comes the rainbow of promise -
               God's Word will always remain true.

When my tasks on this earth are complete, rejoice!
I'm home with our Heavenly Father preparing a place for you;
You must know you are my greatest source of accomplishment and joy -
     I leave knowing you love me, Angels,
          and always remember Mommy loves you!

Our time on this earth is brief and fleeting,
     As Believers we are promised to enter Heaven's door -
          When I go home I will be happy and complete because
          I gave birth to my precious children,
               God's greatest gifts to the world -
               Who could ask for anything more?

© Eurydice S. Stanley

For Grace:

Grace – God's unmerited favor.
We're so thankful for you!

You are Mommy and Daddy's answered prayer,
    God's blessing…
        We'll do all we can to care for you and keep you safe –
            We'll always be there!

You are God's blessing:

    Perfect
    Sweet
    Intelligent
    Bright
    Beautiful
    Ours!

We are so proud of you!
    There is nothing we wouldn't do for you, sweet dove –
        There is no sacrifice too great,
            We love you with an everlasting, unconditional love.

You are our baby –

Grace Audata Stanley –
    Named for God's glory and as a reflection of your parents –
        Daddy Shon's name means "God is Gracious,"
            Grace – God's gift – His unmerited favor –yes, this is you!
                Another name for Mommy Eurydice is Audata
                    Who was a warrior and a queen -
                        Absolutely true, nothing but throne's for you!

You are agape, philial love in the flesh,

    You will forever be God's Grace –

        We'll love you always and all ways!

            Amen!

© Eurydice Stanley

191

Trust in the Lord
with all thine heart,
and not unto thine
own understanding.
In all thy ways
acknowledge Him,
and he shall
direct thy paths.

Proverbs 3:5–6

Epilogue:

The baby learned to "write" watching Mommy all the time,

Soon she had a pad that she'd pull out when she saw mine!

Unfortunately, her prose was not always confined,

And soon her "poems" were scattered throughout the house on walls,
books, bills and anything she could find!

Regardless, it is good to see the family tradition will remain,

And my Sweet Angel will ensure the next generation will be
enlightened while entertained!

To God Be The Glory!

-Grace's Mommy

A Special Initiation...

..."*Repent, and let every one of you be baptized in the name of Jesus Christ for the remission of sins; and you shall receive the gift of the Holy Spirit. For the promise is to your children, and to all who are afar off, as many as the Lord our God will call.*"

Acts 2:38-39

Parenting is a blessing but it definitely has its challenges – I could not imagine trying to do this without God! If you have not sought the Father's Hand and Face, consider the life of both you and your child...God does not promise us anything except for peace and life everlasting, coupled with rest and safe haven in His loving arms.

Romans 3:23 says "For all have sinned, and come short of the glory of God." No one is without sin, yet Christ made the ultimate sacrifice for us, for "while we were yet sinners, Christ died for us." (Romans 5:8). Profess faith, be baptized and find a good church to support your journey as a new Christian, for as Psalm 51:7 states, "Wash me, and I shall be whiter than snow." The Lord will keep you as you "grow in Grace, and in the knowledge of our Lord and Savior Jesus Christ." (II Peter 3:18) God promises to "be faithful unto death, and I will give you the crown of life." (Revelation 2:10).

If you're ready to give your life to Christ, simply pray this prayer:

"Father, I repent of my sins. Please forgive me and lead my life. I ask you into my heart, my life and my world. I know that you are my Lord and Savior, and I thank you for your sacrifices for me. I ask you to guide me and my family, and let us reflect your love here on earth. I thank you and I praise you for your grace and mercy!"

Welcome, friend to the body of Christ! Find a good church to facilitate your growth and guide you on your fantastic journey! I pray your continued strength and blessings! If you gave your life to Christ or have anything that you'd like to share after reading "God's Grace," please send comments to christiangracepublishing@yahoo.com or visit our website at www.christiangracepublishing.com.

May the Lord continue to hold you in His arms!

Continued Blessings!

ABOUT THE AUTHOR

Eurydice Stanley gave her life to Christ at a young age and considers herself blessed to receive His love and guidance in her life. She is proud to be called Mommy by the sweetest girl on earth, Grace Audata Stanley, her 9/11 baby and son Christian, her hurricane blessing from the 2004 Florida Hurricane Season! She thanks God for the gift of poetry, reawakened by her love for her family. Eurydice's poetry has been published in several compilations and recognized by several organizations to include the International Society of Poets, who recognized her in both 2004 and 2005 for Outstanding Achievement in Poetry. She proudly serves her country and the state of Florida as an active duty Major in the National Guard.

Eurydice's career in the military began in 1986 as a Reserve Officer Training Corps (ROTC) 4-year scholarship recipient. She attended Florida Agricultural and Mechanical (FAMU) University as a third generation "Rattler," receiving a B.S. in Public Management, a Certificate of Labor Relations and minoring in Political and Military Science. She graduated with honors and was a Distinguished Military Graduate. Eurydice earned a scholarship to receive her Master's Degree from the University of Minnesota, where she recived a Graduate degree in Industrial Relations specializing in Organizational Development and Speech Communications. She was chosen by the Carlson School of Management to spend a summer studying International Business in Lyon, France at the Universite' Des Enterprise. Eurydice earned her Ph.D. in Psychology and Christian Counseling from Louisiana Baptist University in 2000.

Throughout her active-duty military career, Eurydice has served in numerous Army and Army National Guard positions, to include unit Commander, Equal Opportunity Officer, instructor and advisor, personnel officer, executive officer and public affairs officer. She was blessed to serve throughout the United States and conduct training around the globe as a senior human relations instructor for the Department of Defense. Her greatest honor as an instructor was training South African Troops on cross-cultural communications after Transformation!

Eurydice is an author, motivational speaker, Temperament Therapist and small business owner. She has volunteered counseling services at several facilities and provided training to improve interpersonal relations and cross-cultural understanding for several churches and Christian organizations.

Eurydice is a member of the First Church, First Baptist Church of Mandarin, Florida and numerous organizations. Eurydice enjoys spending time with her wonderful family, reading and making time to take naps whenever possible! She has numerous human relations and cross-cultural articles that have been published and has presented research at several national conferences. She is in the process of publishing her first children's book, *God's Grace II: Psalms of Love for Brown Sugar Princesses* and writing a book of poems for Christian.

The Stanley family currently resides in St. Augustine, Florida.

About the Artists
(Each one is gifted and can be contacted independently)

Robert "Conan" Cason – Originally from Chicago, Illinois, Robert has been friends with Eurydice for 20 years - they served as Army Reserve Officer Training (ROTC) cadets in 1986 at Florida A & M University. Robert specializes in portraits and pastels, and has been nationally recognized for his monochromatic artwork. He served five years in the Air Force and graduated with a B.S. in Biology from Tougaloo College. Robert recently received first place honors for his monochromatic drawings from the Veteran's Administration. Robert's work has been featured in several shows and he is consistently recognized for his attention to detail and exceptional talent. He currently resides in Mississippi.

Samantha Christian – Samantha Marie Christian is the proud daughter of Claudette and Eugene Christian, an American native of Haitian and Trinidadian descent from Homestead, Florida. Currently, Samantha is a Senior scholarship student pursuing a Bachelor's Degree in the area of Fine Arts at Florida A&M University (Tallahassee, FL). She is a proud member of the FAMU Fine Arts Association and also a member of the Clarinet Section in the World Renowned "Marching 100" (Fall 02). Samantha won the 2004 National Historically Black Colleges and Universities (HBCU) Art Competition sponsored by Verizon. She interned at Burrell Communications in Chicago and received cash prizes for both herself and the University totaling more than $37,000.

Peter Hemmer– Pete is a graphic designer living in Melbourne, Florida with his wife Krista, and their triplets Nathaniel, Catherine, and Caroline. He has a Bachelor of Fine Arts from the Savannah College of Art and Design. Aside from graphic design, he is also an illustrator, painter, furniture maker, and habitual Do-It-Yourselfer.

Rick Ulysse – Rick is currently a Senior majoring in art at Florida Agricultural and Mechanical University. He is originally from Haiti. Aside from his beautiful work as an artist, he is also a painter and a sculptor. Rick appreciates the opportunity to share his work with others and looks forward to a successful future in art.

CHRISTIAN GRACE PUBLISHING
QUICK ORDER FORM

Visit our website, ***www.christiangracepublishing.com***, to place orders, identify book signing dates or request speaking engagements and seminars.

Additional books are $19.99

email orders: christiangracepublishing@yahoo.com

Please add sales tax for products shipped to Florida addresses.

Shipping by air:
U.S. $5.00 for first book and $2.50 for each additional book.
International: $11.00 for first book; $7.00 for each additional book
(estimate)

Payment: __ Check __Credit Card: (Number) _____
__ Visa __ MasterCard __ Optima __ American Express __ Discover
Name as it appears on card: _____

Shipping Information:

Name: _____

Address: _____

City: _____ State: _____ Zip: _____

Corporations and interested parties are encouraged to contact Christian Grace Publishing regarding the purchase and donation of copies of God's Grace or other Christian Grace Publications at reduced rates to local shelters and non-profit organizations.
Thank you for sharing the gift of hope and God's love with others!

Christian Grace
PUBLISHING